Wetlands

by Adele D. Richardson

Consultant:
Francesca Pozzi, Research Associate
Center for International Earth Science Information Network
Columbia University

Bridgestone Books
an imprint of Capstone Press
Mankato, Minnesota

Bridgestone Books are published by Capstone Press
151 Good Counsel Drive, P.O. Box 669, Mankato, Minnesota 56002
http://www.capstone-press.com

Library of Congress Cataloging-in-Publication Data
Richardson, Adele, 1966–
   Wetlands/by Adele D. Richardson.
   p. cm.—(The Bridgestone science library)
   Includes bibliographical references and index.
   ISBN 0-7368-0840-X
   1. Wetlands—Juvenile literature. [1. Wetlands. 2. Wetland ecology. 3. Ecology.] I. Title.
II. Series.
QH87.3 .R53 2001
578.768-dc21   00-009808

Summary: Discusses the plants, animals, and climate of a wetland ecosystem.

Editorial Credits
Karen L. Daas, editor; Karen Risch, product planning editor; Linda Clavel, designer and
   illustrator; Heidi Schoof, photo researcher

Photo Credits
Dawn M. Hire/Tom Stack & Associates, 16
Ed Robinson/Tom Stack & Associates, 18
James P. Rowan, 10
Mark Newman/Tom Stack & Associates, 12
PhotoDisc Inc., 5, 7, 9, 11, 13, 15, 17, 19, 21
Robert McCaw, 6, 14
RubberBall Productions, cover, 1
Visuals Unlimited/John Meuser, 20

Table of Contents

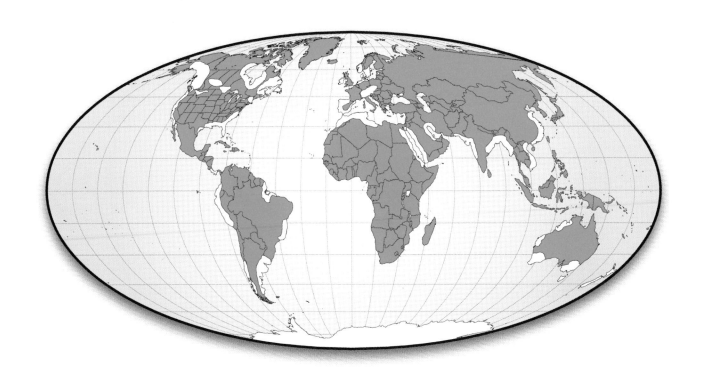

wetlands

- Wetlands are found on every continent except Antarctica.
- More than 1 billion acres (405 million hectares) of wetlands cover Earth.
- About 24 percent of all the world's wetlands are in Canada.
- The Everglades is the largest freshwater marsh in the United States. The Everglades covers about 10,000 square miles (25,900 square kilometers) of land in Florida.
- Rice is a wetland plant. About three billion people eat rice every day.
- Peat is rotted plant material found in some swamps and bogs. It can be dried and burned as fuel.
- Many wetlands contain fresh water. Wetlands near the ocean are filled with salt water.

Wetlands are areas of land that hold water for most of the year. Marshes, swamps, and bogs are wetlands. Some wetlands can be miles wide. Other wetlands are as small as a puddle.

Most marshes start out as ponds with soft, muddy bottoms. Marshes usually have shallow water. Floating and emergent plants grow in marshes. Trees, grasses, and roots sometimes grow in the watery soil. This type of wetland is called a swamp.

Bogs are found in cool areas. A thick layer of plants often floats on top of the water. The plants can be so thick that animals can walk on them. Some bogs are as deep as 30 feet (9 meters).

A wetland may not always stay wet. It can dry out, depending on the season or the time of day. A bog that is wet in spring may be dry during summer. Marshes along the coast are flooded at high tide. During low tide, the water drains out.

Wetlands are like giant sponges. They soak up extra water that might flood roads or houses.

emergent plants

floating aquatics

submergent plants

Layers of a Wetland

Most wetlands have three layers. The layers are described by the kinds of plants that live there. The plants are not the same in every wetland.

Emergent plants make up the top layer of a wetland. These plants and trees grow out of the water. They have roots in the soft, muddy bottom. Reeds and cattails are emergents. Trees, such as the mangrove and the cypress, also are emergents.

Floating aquatics make up the middle layer. These plants float on the water's surface. Duckweeds and water lilies are floating aquatics. Duckweeds look like small leaves. As they float on the water, their roots dangle below the surface.

The bottom layer of a wetland is where submergent plants grow. These plants live completely underwater. Some of these plants are so small that they can be seen only through a microscope. Other plants, such as pondweed and bladderwort, can be seen easily.

Floating aquatics such as duckweeds and water lilies float on the surface of wetlands.

Many kinds of animals live in wetlands. Some animals spend their whole lives there. The most common wetland animals are birds, insects, and snakes.

Ducks and geese from the north often fly to a southern wetland in fall. They spend the winter in the wetland where there is plenty of food and warm temperatures. In the spring, they fly north to breed.

More than 200 different kinds of fish swim in coastal wetlands. Clams, crabs, and shrimp also live there.

Amphibians are common in wetlands. Frogs and toads are amphibians. Amphibians have smooth, wet skin. They can live in or out of water. Amphibians lay their eggs in water.

Larger animals such as raccoons and beavers spend much of their lives in wetlands. They eat the plants and berries that grow there. Beavers make their homes near open water.

Alligators live in wetlands in the southern United States. They stay near the same area their whole lives.

Plants in the Wetlands

More than 5,000 kinds of trees and plants grow in wetlands. Grasses and shrubs are common in marshes. Cattails also grow in marshes. These tall plants have long thin leaves and a fuzzy top that looks like a cat's tail.

Bogs are filled with peat and other mosses. Trees and bushes also grow in bogs. The sundew plant and the pitcher plant catch insects that live in bogs. Many scientists think the plants eat the insects.

Cypress trees grow in swamps. These trees have thick, twisted trunks. Areas of brush called knees grow around the trunk. The knees often are covered with water.

Mangrove trees grow in warm, saltwater swamps. They grow best in shallow water near the ocean. The mangrove tree's thin roots loop over each other. Mangrove trees can reach about 40 feet (12 meters) high.

Plants often grow near the base of cypress trees.

The Wetland Ecosystem

The trees, plants, and animals in a wetland are part of an ecosystem. The water and climate also make up the wetland ecosystem.

Thousands of plants and animals live in a wetland ecosystem. The plants and animals rely on each other for survival. They form a food chain. The food chain starts with tiny plants in the water. These plants make their own food out of sunlight, water, and soil. Insects and small fish eat the tiny plants. Larger animals then eat the plant eaters. When the animals die, their bodies rot and fertilize the soil. Plants use the food in the soil to grow.

The plants and animals in a wetland depend on water to survive. Animals such as frogs and fish need water to live. Many plants and trees can grow only in wetland waters. The trees shelter the animals. In freshwater wetlands, the animals also drink the water.

Canada geese sometimes build their nests on muskrat homes in a wetland.

The Everglades is at the southern tip of Florida. This wetland covers about 10,000 square miles (25,900 square kilometers) of land.

Marshes, swamps, and a river make up the Everglades. Water flows through the Everglades floor. The water runs south from Lake Okeechobee to the Gulf of Mexico. In some places, the river can be as wide as 50 miles (81 kilometers). In other places, the river cannot be seen because it is moving through thick grasses.

Saw grass is a common plant in the Everglades. Saw grass can grow to be 12 feet (3.7 meters) tall. It has sharp edges along each long, narrow blade.

Many animals live in the Everglades. Snakes and alligators are common. Several kinds of insects and birds also make their homes in the Everglades. People sometimes see black bears and panthers there.

Tall grasses nearly hide the flow of water in some parts of the Everglades.

Many of the foods people eat grow in wetlands. Cranberries and rice can only grow there. People often catch crabs and shrimp in saltwater marshes.

Wetlands also help produce the water people drink. Wetland plants act like filters. Their roots and stems collect the dirt at the bottom layer of the wetland. The water seeps past the muddy floor and into the ground. The water underground is pure and fresh. It collects in pools and streams under the earth's surface. People then build wells to collect the groundwater.

People sometimes cut down wetland trees. They make furniture and cabinets from the wood. Cypress wood is valuable because it rarely rots or warps.

People hunt some wetland animals for their skins. People make beaver skins into hats, coats, and gloves. Alligator and snake skins are popular for making belts, boots, and purses.

People plant rice crops in wetlands.

Every year the world loses more wetlands. People fill in wetlands to build roads and houses or to create farmland. Scientists believe that wetland loss will cause more flooding. Water will run off the land instead of soaking into the ground.

Wetland loss also harms drinking water. Some wetland plants can remove poisons from water before it seeps into the ground. This water collects in springs and wells. People then drink this water in their homes.

Animals also suffer when people fill in wetlands. Animals lose their homes. They may starve because their food source is gone.

Governments around the world have passed laws protecting wetlands. The laws say that a certain number of wetlands never can be removed.

People also help protect wetlands. They study wetlands. They teach other people about this valuable ecosystem.

Homes and streets built on wetlands may flood when rain falls. The developed wetlands cannot absorb the rain.

Hands On: Absorb Water

Wetlands absorb rainfall. Areas may flood when people build houses and roads on wetlands. You can learn why areas flood.

What You Need

2 small pans
2 pitchers filled with equal amounts of water
Sponge
Block of wood about the same size as the sponge

What You Do

1. Place the sponge in the bottom of one pan.
2. Pour water from the first pitcher onto the sponge. The sponge is like a wetland. How much water do you need to pour to cover the bottom of the pan?
3. Place the block of wood in the bottom of the second pan.
4. Pour water from the second pitcher onto the wood. The wood is like a house. How much water do you need to pour to cover the bottom of the pan?

You need to pour less water on the wood to cover the bottom of the pan. The wood does not absorb water like the sponge does. Houses also do not absorb water. This is why areas flood when people build houses on wetlands.

Words to Know

amphibian (am-FIB-ee-uhn)—a cold-blooded animal with a backbone

emergent plant (i-MUR-jent PLANT)—a plant that grows out of the water in a wetland

filter (FIL-tur)—to clean water

floating aquatic plant (FLOHT-ing uh-KWAT-ic PLANT)—a plant that floats on the surface of water; the plant's roots usually are underwater.

spring (SPRING)—a place where water rises from underground and becomes a stream

submergent plant (suhb-MUR-jent PLANT)—a plant that lives completely underwater

well (WEL)—a deep hole in the ground; people draw water from a well.

Read More

Cone, Molly. *Squishy, Misty, Damp and Muddy.* The In-Between World of Wetlands. San Francisco: Sierra Club Books for Children, 1996.

Fowler, Allan. *Life in a Wetland.* Rookie Read-About Science. New York: Children's Press, 1998.

Silver, Donald M. *Swamp.* One Small Square. New York: Learning Triangle Press, 1997.

Useful Addresses

Canadian Nature Federation
Suite 606, 1 Nicholas Street
Ottawa, ON K1N 7B7
Canada

National Wetlands Research Center
700 Cajundome Boulevard
Lafayette, LA 70506-3154

Internet Sites

Evergreen Project Adventures—Wetlands
http://mbgnet.mobot.org/fresh/wetlands/index.htm
Interactive Swamp
http://www.auduboninstitute.org/html/interswamp.html
Introduction to Wetlands
http://www.athena.ivv.nasa.gov/curric/land/wetland/
  index.html

Index